# Ur
# The Wineskin of The
# Kingdom

# Understanding The Wineskin of The Kingdom

Dr. Joseph Mattera

μ65

Powered by eGenCo    Generation Culture Transformation
*Specializing in publishing for generation culture change*

eGenCo
824 Tallow Hill Road
Chambersburg, PA 17202, USA
Phone: 717-461-3436
Email: info@micro65.com
Website: www.micro65.com

 facebook.com/egenbooks          pinterest.com/eGenDMP

 youtube.com/egenpub             twitter.com/eGenDMP

 egen.co/blog                    instagram.com/egenco_dmp

Publisher's Cataloging-in-Publication Data
Mattera, Dr. Joseph
Understanding the Wineskin of the Kingdom.;
by Dr. Joseph Mattera. Shannon Johnson, editor.
72 pages cm.
ISBN:     978-1-68019-817-1 paperback
          978-1-68019-818-8 ebook
          978-1-68019-819-5 ebook
1. Religion. 2. God's Law. 3. Societal Transformation. I. Title
2016943224

# TABLE OF CONTENTS

# INTRODUCTION

For many years I have taught on the Kingdom of God, related to the call of the church, to apply the gospel of Jesus to the culture of nations. I have seen God move powerfully in regards to seeing the paradigm of high level Christian leaders in the church and in the marketplace shift from preaching an individual gospel of salvation to the gospel of the Kingdom which has the power to redeem whole spheres of culture, not just individual sinners. (By a sphere of culture I am referring to Economics, Politics, Education, Science, Philosophy, Religion, Law, Media, Arts, and Entertainment and beyond). Although, in the past decade the church has made great strides in understanding the Kingdom, especially in adopting the "Seven Mountain Mandate" (which is a missiological strategy of identifying and reaching the aforementioned spheres of culture). I have been concerned with the fact that our strategies are still fragmented and lack a holistic rubric that enables us to wrap our brain around the big picture.

Understanding and embracing an overarching template can serve as a fundamental starting point that all those engaged in the Seven Mountain Mandate can agree upon. Without a foundation of shared assumptions our strategies will eventually fall short. This is because there has to be general agreement on what societal transformation looks like from the biblical perspective if we are going to have the same objectives. This is the thesis of this book.

For the first seventeen years of my walk with God, my understanding of the Kingdom of God had to do with merely manifesting the power of God that pointed to the Kingdom as Jesus taught in Matthew 12:28 (as well as the gifts of the Spirit as shown in 1 Corinthians 12:4-8). My focus for the first seventeen years was on bringing revival to the nations through much fasting, prayer and seeing God demonstrate His power to the unbelieving world. I also put a lot of personal focus on seeking God and knowing God, pouring over the Scriptures to understand God's ways, and practicing the spiritual disciplines (Read Richard Foster's book "A Celebration Of Discipline" for an idea of what I mean). When I came to understand the message of the Kingdom of God in a fuller sense (in 1995), I began to study how the Kingdom of God impacted nations and systems not just churches and individual people. I began to see that the starting point of all ministry is Genesis 1:26-28 which some scholars call "The Cultural Mandate". I found that this portion of Scripture revealed the first covenant God made with humanity, Adam, which then became the starting point for all biblical interpretation and the genesis to understanding all subsequent covenants. I discovered, without this covenant, we cannot understand any other covenant including the New Covenant because Jesus was called the last Adam (1 Corinthians 15:45). This means that we cannot understand His ministry and purpose unless we go back to the covenant God made with the first Adam. Even the Great Commission found in Matthew 28:19-20 takes upon a whole new meaning when we understand the Cultural Mandate (Genesis 1:26-28). For example, when you interpret all succeeding covenants with the Cultural Mandate, then you understand Matthew 29:19 to refer to the believer's call to disciple whole nations, not just individual ethnic people. Hence, many scholars believe that the Great Commission passage in Matthew is the New Testament equivalent to the Cultural Mandate given to Adam in Genesis 1:26-28. This new understanding revolutionized my understanding of Scripture, changed my preaching, and even changed our local church (Resurrection Church of New York).

However, in spite of this paradigmatic theological change, I never let go of my previous practices of seeking God, fasting, praying, believing God to manifest His power, and the spiritual disciplines. If you sat next to me on a plane and you understood theology, you would think I was schizophrenic because I might have a biography of John Hyde (the great prayer warrior of the early 20th century) and a book by my favorite Christian philosopher, Cornelius Van Til.

Furthermore, I have found that many of those who preach on the Kingdom of God rarely emphasize prayer, fasting and seeking God. I have found that leaders in the body of Christ often fall into one of two categories: either a leader is an 'activist' who is devoted to a cause like traditional marriage or pro life issues/ or they are a 'pietist' who focuses more on the power of intercession to change a nation. Often, the activist makes fun of the 'pietist' and calls them mystical, and the 'pietist' believe the activist is just a person full of ambition who is trying to bring God's kingdom on their own efforts. In the following pages, I hope to bring both activist and 'pietist' together. I hope to present a rubric of the Kingdom of God that will enable both the First and Second Testaments to be woven together in such a way that it will synergize the revival and reformation camps, the mystic and activist, and those who emphasize individual holiness with those who desire to see societal and systemic change.

Dr. Joseph Mattera

# CHAPTER ONE

# TRANSFORMATION AS DEFINED BY GOD

*² And it shall come to pass in the last days, that the mountain of the LORD's house shall be established in the top of the mountains, and shall be exalted above the hills; and all nations shall flow unto it. ³ And many people shall go and say, Come ye, and let us go up to the mountain of the LORD, to the house of the God of Jacob; and he will teach us of his ways, and we will walk in his paths: for out of Zion shall go forth the law, and the word of the Lord from Jerusalem. ⁴ And he shall judge among the nations, and shall rebuke many people: and they shall beat their swords into plowshares, and their spears into pruning hooks: nation shall not lift up sword against nation, neither shall they learn war any more.* (Isaiah 2:2-4 KJV**)**

It is easy for those of us who preach on the Kingdom of God to teach that God wants to transform nations, however, we need to have a common definition of what that looks like. Merely using the word "transformation" is ambiguous and if we do not have a common definition of the meaning of "transformation" then our objective and goals will not coincide with one another. This passage in Isaiah is extremely important because it gives a clear definition of what national transformation looks like from God's point of view. In this passage, we notice that there is a Mountain of God. In the bible, this word is often used as a metaphor to depict either God's majesty, Kingdom, or nations and empires. In this particular passage it indicates both God's Kingdom and nations of the world.

In this beautiful picture, God is showing that in the last days, His Mountain will be lifted up above all other mountains, and that the nations of the world will come to the mountain of the Lord to learn His Ways and for Him to teach them His Laws. Thus, in this context, they cannot know His ways regarding how to function as a nation without knowing His laws. His laws reveal His ways when it comes to civil government and spheres of culture. This has vast implications! This means that we who preach on the Kingdom of God and penetrate the Seven Mountains of Culture need to understand and study the laws of God so we can disciple our nation.

Furthermore, verse two calls the Mountain of God the 'Mountain of the Temple (or assembly) of the Lord' which puts the true believing church, who is called the 'temple of God' in 1 Corinthians 6, *in* the Mountain of God. The church is not the Kingdom of God but is in the Kingdom as the main agent of change and/or His representative to the world. Consequently, if the church is in the Kingdom mountain and not in the mountains of culture or nations that look to God for His Law, then the church is not in the so-called "religion mountain" as many seven mountain practitioners believe. The church is not in the same mountain as the Buddhists, Muslims,

Mormons, Hindi's and nominal Christians. Further-more, according to Colossians 1:13, when we are born again God translates us out of the kingdom of darkness and places us into the Kingdom of His Son. This means, whether we believe it or not, true believers are already in the Kingdom of God positionally. Which again puts the true church in the mountain of God and not in the religion mountain. What I am not saying here is that the institutional, organized church is over the nations, but individual believers who make up the visible (spiritual) church, irrespective of denominational affiliation, are in the mountain of God. This means that, the main call of the local church is to serve as an equipping center in which believers are raised up from within the Kingdom Mountain and sent into all the other mountains to teach them the ways and laws of God. This is why God has called the five primary ministry gifts to equip the saints for the work of the ministry. According to Ephesians 4:10, the context demands that we redefine the "work of the ministry" to include the "filling up of all things" which was the purpose of the resurrection and ascension of Christ. In light of the ascension, God has given the church these five ministry gifts to train believers to serve God in every sphere of culture to fill up all things and bring Kingdom government to the whole earth. That is to say, the five ministry gifts are not just to prepare other preachers, pastors and plan church planting, but are to train architects, plumbers, painters, composers, econo-mists, politicians, mothers and fathers and beyond, to bring God's Kingdom presence and rule to every domain in which they serve.

The following diagram will make this concept clearer:

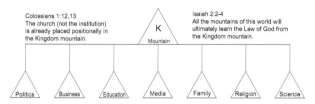

7 Cultural Mountains: Politics, Business, Education, Media, Family, Religion, Science

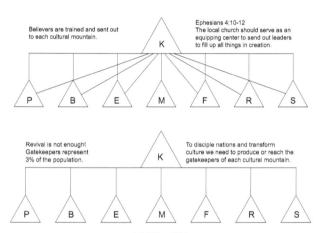

2 Corinthians 10:3-5
To reach or equip the gatekeepers of each cultural mountain we need to have a biblical worldview in each sphere.

As you can see from these three diagrams, the people of God are equipped and sent by the church to bring the law of God to the mountains of culture.

Before we go any further, I want to make sure I help define further the concept of the Kingdom of God as it is portrayed in scripture. This we will do in the next chapter.

# CHAPTER TWO

# DEFINING THE KINGDOM OF GOD

From my perspective, the Kingdom of God is the rule of God that emanates from the throne of God (the throne of God is where His personal presence is in heaven). The Kingdom of God rules over all, not just over the true church. There are two aspects of this rule: 1) the Kingdom of God sovereignly rules over all. In a general sense, Psalm 22:28 teaches that God rules over all the nations which is also the theme of the book of Daniel (Daniel 4:32-35); 2) In addition to the general rule of God, the Kingdom of God can be also be personally manifest to affect change in the lives of people. This is what Jesus meant when He said that when He cast out demons it was to demonstrate that the Kingdom of God had come in the midst of the people (Matthew 12:28). This is also what He meant when He taught believers to pray for His Kingdom to come and His will to be done on earth as it is in heaven (Matthew 6:6-9). In the first kind of general rule, God created the natural laws that maintain and hold the whole universe together so it doesn't collapse into chaos (Colossians 1:17). In the second kind of rule, it is not just God maintaining the physical laws and systems of the universe but God manifesting Himself in a personal way by His Spirit through His people (Mark 16:15-20, Acts 28:5-10 and more).

The macro theme of the New Testament is not the church but the Kingdom of God which points us back to the cultural mandate of Genesis 1:26-28.

When Jesus taught us how to pray He did not tell us to pray for His church to come but for His Kingdom to come and His will to be done. Since the Kingdom of God includes all of the created order, the main call of the church is not just to fill large buildings with people on Sunday mornings- but to equip the saints to go outside the four walls of the building and bring God's Kingdom power, principles and rule to every sphere of society. Jesus called the church "The salt of the earth and the light of the world", (Matthew 5:13-16) -not the salt of the church and the light of the church. Furthermore, the word Kingdom means 'the King's domain'. This implies that the Kingdom of God is all about every aspect of culture aligning itself with the rule of the King of the kingdom. This is why Jesus is called the "King of kings and Lord of lords" (Revelation 19:16). Notice, Jesus is called the 'King of kings' not the 'king of the church'. He is not the king of the church but the 'head' of the church. To the world He is their Judge and King, but to the church He is their elder brother, groom and Son of the Father who crowned Him King of kings and Lord of lords. Jesus is the King of every earthly king, President of every president, Governor of every governor, Mayor of every mayor and CEO of every CEO. Hence, we cannot escape the fact that Jesus did not come to the earth merely to die for our sins, but also to realign the whole of creation back under His control and domain (Colossians 1:20). This is why John the Baptist, Jesus and Paul preached the Kingdom of God (Read Matthew 3:2; Mark 1:15; Acts 28:31).

This is also why Jesus told Pilate it was for this reason He was born (John 18:37).

Finally, the reason why Jesus taught us to pray for His kingdom to come and His will to be done on earth as it is in heaven (notice the words 'on earth') is because His focus for the church was not heaven but the earth. The bible is not a book about heaven but is the most practical book ever written about how to steward the earth under the lordship of Christ. Furthermore, His point of reference was heaven. Why did Jesus say that we should bring His will on earth as it is in heaven, even though the bible doesn't shed much light on what heaven looks like, and how the people who live there function? The reason is, in heaven, Satan and his angels who rebelled against God's rule, were thrown out and their rebellion was squelched. Thus, the mission of God on the earth for the church is to bring the created order back under the Lordship of Jesus as the King of kings and Lord of lords. Of course, the title King of kings also has vast political implications because Jesus as the King of kings shows that He is the only true King of the world and that every other king and president should bow to Him and obey Him. This is why Psalm 2:8-12 is so important to know if we are going to understand the purpose of the first coming of Christ. It was not just to be a savior of believers but also to be the Lord, not just of the church but also of every nation, which is the Father's gift to the Son in the climax of human history.

# CHAPTER THREE

# REACHING THE MOUNTAINS OF CULTURE THROUGH THE MOUNTAIN OF GOD

If the church is to serve as an equipping center to reach all of the mountains of culture, then she needs to be more concerned with sending people into the world as salt and light than merely getting people to attend Sunday services.

Not only that, but this also challenges pastors to have a biblical worldview in all the main spheres of culture so that they will know how to disciple and equip those that attend their congregation

The best way to immediately impact culture is to have a 'top down' approach, which will be the subject of the next chapter. What I mean by that is to have a goal to reach the top gatekeepers of each of the cultural mountains (E.G. Music, Art, Entertainment, Media, Politics, Law, Business, Family, Religion, Science). However, we cannot only have a 'top down' approach in which we attempt to reach those presently serving as gatekeepers. We also need to have a 'bottom up' approach in which we train and equip our young people in a biblical worldview according to the particular sphere of influence to which they are assigned. Scripture gives us principles in music, art, science, politics, law, business, and economics that the pastor should understand in a general sense, so that they can equip these promising young people with a proper template. As someone who has served as a local church pastor for more than 30 years in NYC, the best way to do this, is to take about ten percent of the most promising young people starting with the age of sixteen, and pouring into them biblical worldview training in each of the major cultural spheres. This way, by the time they get to college, they will understand how to interpret the various concepts that comes to them from the secular humanists. Many young people adapt a humanistic worldview in our churches because the Body of Christ only teaches them things related to individual salvation but neglects the cultural spheres. Unfortunately, when these young people sit in the classrooms and are inculcated with secular humanism, they will believe this philosophy because they are ill equipped. The word of God is comprehensive, congruent, and cohesive, the three C's when it comes to salvation and redemption, but it is equally potent when it comes to answering the question "how shall we now live?" in light of the Kingdom of God. Unless our young people are equipped in the area of these 'three C's', related to all of life (all the cultural spheres), when humanism is presented in a comprehensive manner it will make more logical sense to them, and our Christian kids will adopt this pagan worldview.

Consequently, as I said previously, this challenges pastors and leaders to study the scriptures in regards to having a biblical worldview in all of the major cultural spheres so that they can teach and equip their young people. God has called the church to have a multi-generational plan to send our children into the world to become the world's greatest statesmen and problem solvers. It may take ten to twenty years, but if we take the time to pour into these promising young people they will become the gatekeepers of tomorrow who will begin to displace satanic systems with godly systems aligned under biblical principles. Practically speaking, I tell pastors to take these promising young people aside to train them because, if we dig down deep regarding the biblical worldview every Sunday, we will begin to lose the majority of people who do not feel called to be a leader in the cultural spheres. On Sundays, we should continue to preach pastoral messages with a kingdom perspective that minister to the individuals and families in our churches; but at the same time, disciple the remnant called to be cultural change agents.

This is the best and most sustainable method of shifting culture to the values of the Kingdom of God since it is based on nurturing leadership from the ground up who will have a strong biblical foundation. These same young people will most likely also keep a strong connection with their pastor and local church, which can sustain them when they enter the rat race of political business.

In closing, this is the same method that king Nebuchadnezzar of Babylon used in the first chapter of Daniel when they picked the choice Hebrew children, changed their names, and gave them the best pagan education possible to prepare them for cultural leadership. If a pagan king like Nebuchadnezzar could be successful in nurturing Daniel to be a great prophet/statesman, how much more can our churches do the same with the most promising young people in our churches!

# CHAPTER FOUR

# WHY REVIVAL IS NOT ENOUGH TO SHIFT SECULAR CULTURE

It is a mistake to believe that secular culture will shift because of a church revival or a societal awakening. Often, we as believers think the key to societal transformation is to convert masses of people. But the truth is, everyone is led by the decisions of the approximately 3-5% of people who make up the cultural elite in a society. Thus, the only way to affect cultural change is to convert the elite who formulate culture in every sphere of society.

Second, it is a mistake to think that political victories will bring transformation. For example, abortion was legalized in 1973 yet the fight still rages on; same-sex marriage has been legalized but the battle will never stop; homosexuality has been normalized by art, media and entertainment yet much of the rank and file of America still reject it.

The truth is that politics is only one expression of societal power. We need to influence the other mind-molding sectors of society if we are going to dictate the direction of culture. For example, we need to infiltrate and influence the Ivy League universities, especially Harvard, Yale, and Princeton to change public policy, education, science, views on economics, etc. We need to influence major news outlets like the New York Times, CNN, MTV, etc. and not write only for Christian newspapers and appear only on Christian television stations like TBN.

Hence, we need to train the ekklesia (Greek word for 'Church' in Matthew 16) to take the lead, not only in church related ministry, but by actually being professors, board members and chief executives of leading elite entities in art, music, entertainment, education, media and public policy (for example, the Hoover Institute and the Manhattan Institute).

We need to distinguish between merely just assembling together which is to synagogue (episynagoge) as found in Hebrews 10:25, the common function and conceptual view of most church leaders, from the Ekklesia which in its classical and biblical usage means to come together to rule. (Sort of like the parliament or congress to decide matters of public policy, the way it was used in Acts 19:21-41.)

Having famous athletes and entertainers getting saved and giving testimonies is not nearly enough. We need revivals and multi-generational strategies to place our leading thinkers and practitioners in the highest levels of highbrow culture, like God did with Daniel and the three Hebrew youths in Babylon, if we are going to see societal change (read Daniel chapter 1).

Third, we need to nurture and/or convert those who are part of the emerging "creative class" who comprise between 12-30% of the population but have by far the most wealth producers and will drive the economy for generations to come. Those in the creative class used to be considered mavericks and non-conformists but are now part of the mainstream and part of a movement that has radically shifted the future of business and culture! Some of the characteristics of this new creative class-driven economy are:

Businesses are moving towards creative urban centers such as New York City, Seattle and San Francisco. Thus, geography is essential because it is moving from corporate-driven to people-driven; companies are moving to where the most creative people live, not just where there are tax incentives and highways.

Typical hierarchical structures are quickly becoming a thing of the past. New companies accommodate creative people who like to be self-managed, set their own hours, and are free to think, create, and dress informally. Autonomy, diversity and self-identity are valued more than conformity, conservatism, and 'groupthink'. These people like to play at work and work at play; the lines between work and leisure are becoming more blurred.

Top-down autocratic leadership, which expects people to just follow orders and not think on their own, is no longer effective. Companies are now encouraging creative people to join their ranks who are semi-autonomous and self-managed with leverage to set their own hours.

A person being loyal to one community and one company for the rest of his or her life is a thing of the past. People are now moving from company to company every several years based on new opportunities to accommodate their interests, increased skills, need to meet new friends, creativity, and desire for change and advancement. Because of the information age we are in, there are now also virtual communities with much information changing and being exchanged every day. This is making it harder to have cohesive communities and set societal norms which results in fragmentation and postmodernism.

Diversity is in, yet conservative values are respected but not the 'norm'. Only 23% of the families in the United States are nuclear families. Alternate family structures are now becoming the 'norm'.

(Read Richard Florida's book *"The Rise of the Creative Class"* which delves into and fully unpacks everything I wrote in this last point).

## How should the church respond?

The church should build authentic communities to model the city of God before we attempt to transform the city of man. We have to honor unity, family, and kingdom unity with churches in our regions before we can transform the pagan systems and cultures around us.

World-changers need to experience creativity, leadership, covenant, unity, purpose and kingdom power in the church community (ekklesia) so they can be adequately discipled to recreate these things in the secular arenas to which they are called. Senior leaders need to transition away from top down autocratic leadership style approaches if they want to attract the creative class to their church.

We need to start investing a good portion of our monies towards educating and cultivating the most creative people in our churches and place them in every leadership sphere of society, starting with the ivy league schools. Consequently, we need a multi-generational approach. We need to recapture the classical meaning of Ekklessia as used in Athens and in Acts 19 when it referred to (a secular entity) assembling together for rulership as contrasted with merely assembling like the word to synagogue.

We have to understand that prayer, fasting, and revival only among masses of people will not shift the culture; similar to how the 1857 Prayer Revival, the Azusa Street Revival in 1906, and the numerous Voice of Healing, Toronto Blessing and Pensacola renewals have not shifted culture. Only when revivals affect cultural thinkers who prove to be influential like Marx, Lenin, Freud, Darwin, and Bill Gates -will culture shift. This is not to say that prayer, fasting and revival are not important. Of course, reaching and renewing masses of people and Christians is important to spread the gospel and save souls, but in this book we are discussing how to truly experience societal transformation.

Even as we examine the Scriptures we see that God has used people that were already in high places of authority and/or culture before a nation was transformed.

As we do a quick review, we find:

- Moses already was a prince in Egypt before he was called to confront Egypt and deliver the people of God out of slavery.
- Daniel was serving as a top political advisor to the King of Babylon (Nebuchadnezzar) and later as a prime minister in Persia, which positioned him to speak truth to power and transform culture.
- Nehemiah was the cupbearer of the King of Persia, which enabled him to receive the favor necessary to rebuild the walls of Jerusalem.

- Samuel was the first in a line of great Jewish prophets who also served as the political judge of the nation.
- David, Samuel's protégé, may have been a great psalmist but he also became a king.

Finally, all the great prophets (Isaiah, Jeremiah, Elijah, Elisha, Micaiah, Ahijah, Amos, etc.) did not just prophesy to small crowds of people in the temple or synagogue; they had access to political and cultural elites, even to the highest political office of the land. We need to cultivate kingdom prophets who speak truth to power outside the four walls of the church.

Even church history reiterates this. For example, it took the conversion of Roman Emperor Constantine to legalize Christianity, placing it in a position to transform the whole empire. St. Augustine was first the professor of rhetoric for the imperial court, the most visible academic position in the Latin world, before converting and becoming the Bishop of Hippo, which put him on the platform to become the greatest theologian and thinker of his age. In 800 AD it was Christian Emperor Charlemagne who laid the groundwork for the first cathedral universities, which were the forerunners for all modern universities. The two primary leaders of the Protestant Reformation: Martin Luther and John Calvin, received educations that included vast knowledge of the classics, not just the Bible. Calvin at one point actually considered becoming a lawyer. The two leaders of the First Great Awakening (that saved England from the destruction that France suffered later in their revolution, and was also the impetus for the American Revolution), John

Wesley and George Whitefield, not only knew the scriptures but also graduated from Oxford. Thus they were already positioned to have the respect of the top decision makers of society. Furthermore, Whitefield's American counterpart Jonathan Edwards was a graduate of Princeton and later became the president of Princeton. The abolition of slavery in the British Empire was affected by the Clapham Sect, which included William Wilberforce, who was a parliamentarian and a close friend of William Pitt the Prime Minister of England and many other cultural and political leaders. The Second Great Awakening in the United States was led by Charles Finney, a capable lawyer whose preaching was able to relate to many lawyers, judges and top decision makers in culture. He affected the course of our nation that led to the abolition of slavery, the implementation of child labor laws, women's suffrage and many other things. As we have already stated, the Azusa Street Revival and other 20th century revivals did not have significant cultural impact because they primarily converted masses of people without touching the cultural elite and top decision makers of society.

We must understand the delicate balance between infiltrating and engaging the cultural elites and highbrows of society without losing our souls and becoming elites in heart and purpose. The "Beatitudes" of Matthew 5-7 teach us how to interface with others in our communities.

The church needs to learn how to avoid the extremes of the Christian Right, Christian Left, and the 'pietists' who avoid cultural engagement altogether. The Christian Right thinks the answer is only political. This approach clothes the gospel of Christ with a particular political party and pits us against people in the world who we are trying to save. This results in us trying to exert power and control people through legal means and changing laws. Although I believe the laws of a state should be based on the Ten Commandments, and that the law is a school master that brings conviction of sin (and is an emblem of what a particular society values), in and of itself the law is a very weak line of defense because of the vicissitudes of democratic elections. This approach also smacks of Constantinianism. (When the fourth century Roman Emperor Constantine was converted to Christianity and seemed to compel the masses within his empire to adopt the Christian faith as their own). Although Christianity became the favorite religion of the Roman Empire in the 4th century, this resulted in weakening the church from within because unconverted pagans joined the Christian community without abandoning their lifestyles and core beliefs. The Christian Left only accommodates the gospel to the prevailing culture, which results in losing the biblical distinctions of salt and light. A church that recognizes same-sex marriage and whose values reflect the world's more than the Ten Commandments, has already lost its soul and reason for existing as a Christian community. The 'pietists' and Anabaptists take the approach that the church should only build alternative sub-cultures that don't engage or affirm the prevailing culture. The kingdom alternative is to take the approach of the Celtic Church in the 6th to 8th centuries. They incorporated the Anabaptist strategy of building an alternative community that was a model for the pagan communities they lived among. However, they also recognized

God's favor upon His created order (God blessed His creation and called it good) which many theologians refer to as common grace. Thus, their communities of faith embraced the non-believing communities, loved them, and won them to Christ by demonstrating the gospel in everyday life. The church is called to build what James Davison Hunter, in his book *To Change the World*, describes as communities of faith that both affirm the good in their surrounding societal structures (hospitals, art, police, transportation, commerce, music, science, education, etc.) while also demonstrating the antithesis against that which is sinful and corrupt, not necessarily only in word but how we live our lives as Christ followers. Davidson also calls this approach having a "faithful presence" and bases it on what God prophesied to the Jewish exiles in Babylon and Persia in Jeremiah 29:4-7. In that passage, God told the exiles to build houses, build families, settle down and live normal lives, seek the welfare of the city they lived in, and pray to the Lord for those around them, because as the city was blessed they would be blessed.

The church must maintain a balance between honoring the traditions of the church and relating to contemporary culture. We are also called to model the power and blessing of the traditional nuclear family and marriage if we are going to be the antithesis to the fragmentation and curse of the alternate family structures of the present pagan world system.

We also have to repent for separating the gospels from the epistles in our approach to evangelism and discipleship that has resulted in attempting to change the world outside the master plan of Jesus for world evangelization, which is the local church. This is why the culture is continuing to decline in the United States in spite of the fact that the United States has 33 percent of the population claiming to be evangelical as well as more mega churches and gospel proclamation in its history!

The master or methodological plan for evangelism is not found in the gospels but in Acts and the Epistles. The gospels were written after the epistles were written to give context to the churches for the gospel story, not the other way around! Thus, Acts 1:1 teaches us that all Jesus began to say and do was to be fleshed out in its fullness by the creation of kerygmatic (or proclaiming) communities that would be responsible for converting the Roman Empire in three hundred years. This is what Jesus planned all along! (For more on this read two encyclicals from Jeff Reed : "Kerygmatic Communities: Evangelism and the early church" and "From Jesus to the Gospels"; go to BILD.ORG )

In the New Testament, there was no separation between missions, evangelism, helping the poor and nurturing disciples from the local church as you can see from reading the epistles.

Thus, planting simple local churches that participate in complex apostolic networks that function as kerygmatic communities in every community of the world- that trains, and utilizes commissioned elite (special forces) marketplace ekklesias, that function as a shadow government in every elite sphere- without being disconnected from the local church -is the key to world transformation.

Where you have complex apostolic networks, you have less need for para-church organizations that are not rooted in the local church because local churches that band together to train leaders and do missions can compensate for each other's lack.

In summary: If we are going to transform culture we need to engage and shift the influencers toward biblical values at the highest levels in every major sphere of society. We cannot only reach masses of people and change political elections. If we don't reach the 3-5% who are the decision makers, then we will never reach our goals of societal transformation.

We also need to bring back the centrality of the local church that function as kerygmatic communities in association with complex apostolic networks (for more info on complex apostolic networking, read Jeff Reed's encyclical "The Churches of the first century"; BILD.org).

As we think about the Scripture in Jeremiah 29:4-7 we realize the most important thing we are called to do is to live exemplary lives that are good witnesses to our surrounding communities. We need to embrace, serve and love our cities and communities, while at the same time train our children and those with the greatest potential in our churches to take the lead at the gates of every sphere of society. The battle for transformation is a multi-generational battle!

CHAPTER FIVE

# THE FIVE JURISDICTIONS THAT GOVERN THE MOUNTAINS OF CULTURE

In scripture there are five basic jurisdictions (or governments) God has set up in His Kingdom: **Self Government, Family Government, Voluntary Associations, Civic Government, Religious or Church government**

Each of these five have separate and distinct functions, although they are to function interdependently. To show how much the body of Christ has been brainwashed by the secular humanists, all we have to do is ask the typical believer "What is the first thing you think about when I say the word government?" Most people will say the name of their president, governor or mayor, which shows that the average believer has embraced the  humanist view of the large central government controlling all five jurisdictions of culture. Unless this is changed, the church cannot hope to displace pagan systems that abound in the present political systems of the world including the USA. Whenever a political leader says that the solution for the ills of our culture is the "Government" then you know that they have drunk out of the fount of secular humanism, whether they claim to be a Christian or not.

To show how far we have fallen in our nation from the biblical worldview, all you have to do is purchase an 1827 version of Webster's Dictionary and look up the definition for the word "government" and you will find that the first answer it gives is not political but self-government. Now if you look in a typical contemporary dictionary, the first answer to this definition is political government and self-government is nowhere to be found in its answer!

## *Self Government*

This refers to the fact that people are responsible for their own life. Galatians 6:7,8 teaches us that "whatsoever a man sows that shall he also reap". The book of Proverbs is filled with passages of scripture that deal with human, individual responsibility. St. Paul says in II Timothy 3:10 "that if a man doesn't work then he should not eat"! Contrary to the biblical worldview of self responsibility is the humanistic modern view which is: genetic determinism (my behavior is determined by genetics, not by my personal choices), environmental determinism (a person is the victim of his community and or environment and not totally responsible for his choices), psychological determinism (a person thinks and acts the way his parents programmed him or her to act). Although scripture teaches that all of these previous three points impact the lives of individuals, often the secular humanists go too far and make every person a victim with no real choice to improve their life.

Other passages that relate to personal responsibility include: Jeremiah 31:29,30; Ezekiel 18:20; John 3:16; Acts 17:30,31; the whole book of Proverbs.

## *Family Government*

By family government we refer to the fact that the scriptures teach that parents have the jurisdiction over their under age children as opposed to the state controlling them.

Scriptures related to family government include: Genesis 2:24; Numbers 1:52; Joshua 7:13,14, 16-18; Acts 16:31; Matthew 28:19 (heads of households are baptized first); Ephesians 5:22-25; 6:1-4; Acts 5 (Ananias and Sapphira).

The bible teaches parents in Deuteronomy 6:6,7 are to diligently teach their children which also means that the primary responsibility of educating young people falls into the hands of the parents of these children as opposed to the socialist view that education is the responsibility of the state. It is this kind of socialistic viewpoint that has led to a nation like Germany to make it illegal for parents to home school their children!

## *Voluntary Associations/Business*

By voluntary associations we are referring to the right of individuals to band together to conduct business and or an individual who has the right to conduct business and make a living.

Scriptures dealing with business can include the following passages:

James 3:13; 5:4; Isaiah 65:21-23; 1 Kings 4:25, 1 Corinthians 9:7, Matthew 25:14-30.

In this passage found in Matthew 25, Jesus praises the person who invests their money and makes interest; hence, by implication, Jesus, by the use of this parable was endorsing good business practices that involved making a profit.

## *Civic*

By civic government we are referring to political leadership. Scriptures dealing with the purpose of political leadership include: Proverbs 8:15, 16, 20; Romans 13:1-7; I Timothy 2:1-5 (These passages show that the primary role of civic government is to keep order and promote freedom, justice and peace);

Generally speaking issues like health care, the environment, and caring for the poor was in the hands of families and the local churches (read the next point for more clarification on this).

## *Church Government*

God put extraordinary responsibility into the hands of the Levites which are a type of the New Covenant believer while the priest can also be a type of the five ministry gifts found in Ephesians 4:11, because they serve God's covenant people in presenting them to God equipped and mature (1 Peter 2:8-9). In Leviticus chapters 11 -15, we find that the priests were responsible to enforce laws related to diet, money and taxation, land, health care, the environment and home safety. Much of these laws have been taken over by the civic government. Scripture related to other duties of the church include: Matthew 16:18-19; Matthew 18:15-17; (these passages in Matthew deal primarily with church government)

Ephesians 4:10-11. (This passage deals with the five fold ministry being called to equip the saints). In 1 Corinthians 6, the apostle Paul also gives the churches the right to conduct their own trials to settle their own in house family issues so that the secular courts would not expose their sins to the unbelieving world.

## Unbiblical Overlap

When any one of these five governments over reaches and lords it over one or all of the other four governments, it is guilty of unbiblical overlap between the jurisdictions. Example: today's socialist concept of Messianic Statism in which the state teaches the people that it alone has the right to rule over all the other jurisdictions. The following are a sample of modern day examples of unbiblical overlap:

The state violates self-government when they tell people they can't pray in a school or in a graduation ceremony. The state violates family government by charging a death or inheritance tax, (its double taxation as well as the fact that they are taking a large part of the inheritance from children) marriage tax, past welfare laws penalizing marriage, progressive income tax (read 1 Samuel 8:11-18 for a list of messianic state violations against the individual and families). Another example is in Germany where they take children away from parents if they home school them because they say parents can teach their children a parallel view of society.

The state violates the realm of voluntary associations and business when they overreach in environmental laws, excessive zoning and fees for permits as well as excessive taxation.

The state violates the jurisdiction of the Church when it requires them to get a 501c3 for taxation because it puts churches under jurisdiction of the state. Hence, churches under such jurisdiction are prohibited (contrary to the first amendment) to promote political views, and in the future, bible believing churches may be closed down or fined if they refuse to recognize or perform same sex weddings.

## *Biblical Overlap*

The state is not violating the jurisdiction of self-government when a person breaks the law; for example, if you murder somebody or if you are caught stealing from somebody, you lose your right of self-freedom and civic government has the right to incarcerate you.

The state has the right to intervene in family government if parents refuse to take care of the basic necessities of their children and or manage their child. In cases of severe neglect and abuse, a state agency has the right to remove children from their home because of these reasons and or juvenile criminal activity.

The state can intervene with the jurisdiction of a business and close it down if it operates a sweatshop or discriminates based on race, is involved in tax evasion, or has serious safety violations that endanger the life of it's workers to name a few.

The state can and should intervene in church affairs in cases where there is sexual or mental abuse, financial fraud, etc.

# CHAPTER SIX

# THE FOUR STEPS TO PUBLIC POLICY

To show the importance of the jurisdiction of religion (which the church fits into) I am now going to share the four basic steps to public policy. This will show the importance of the role theology and religious belief have upon cultural formation.

First of all, the word culture comes from the word "cultus" which means religion. This is why the word 'cult' refers typically to an aberrant religious sect. Hence, even the word culture is a religious word because from the beginning God placed His throne at the center of all cultures. This is the original reason why even to this day, many villages, towns and cities have a church with a high steeple at the center of their population. This is also why the Muslims attempt to build a mosque with a tower higher than all the surrounding buildings. It is a sign that their religion is the most influential power in their area and that one day their religion will be the religion of all the local inhabitants (in their view).

Consequently, there are generally four steps to public policy for all cultures: **Theology or religion, Philosophy of life, Political theory, The formation of laws and public policy.**

## *The Importance of Theology in Culture*

The prevailing religious view in a village or city will organically give birth to a philosophy of life because people will invariably ask themselves the question, "How shall we now live in light of our religious beliefs?" (by the way, humanism, atheism and agnosticism qualifies as a religion in this context).

Thus, if the church abandons culture, then instead of the first point saying biblical theology, we will have to replace it with secular humanism, atheism, communism, socialism or any other ism that is the prevailing belief system of that people group. This is exactly what has happened in the nations of the West which is why we presently have a philosophy of life and laws that are anti-biblical.

Of course this was not the case in the founding years of the United States. Since the church understood these four steps, they created Christian universities like Harvard, Yale, Princeton, and Columbia to train the future gatekeepers of culture. As a matter of fact, they believed that theology was the queen of all of the other sciences, which motivated Christians to found 108 of the first 110 colleges in the USA. They correctly believed that every other discipline had to circle around theology so that every leader in politics, business, economics and policy would be grounded in a biblical worldview that would serve as the interpretive grid for all data. Therefore, in light of the above, we can see why the United States prospered so quickly and how it was considered a nation influenced primarily by the Judeo Christian worldview.

Out of theology arises a philosophy of life which eventually gave birth to the two founding documents of the USA, the Declaration of Independence and the U.S. Constitution which were both grounded in the Judeo Christian belief that human rights come only from God. The U.S. Constitution also asserts that (because human nature is so wicked by nature), we also need checks and balances and a separation of powers between the executive, judicial and congressional branches of government .

## *Having a Philosophy for Life*

As said prior, out of the prevailing religious worldview people begin to ask the question, "How shall we now live in light of our theology or religious beliefs?" Hence, theology and/or religion is the foundation for every philosophy of life under the sun. When the church abandoned culture after the U.S. Civil War, they gave opportunity to the secular humanists to capture every institute of higher learning including all of the major universities- so that by the 1920's secular humanism was the prevailing worldview of the upcoming gate-keeper elites. By the 1960's these adherents to secular humanism took the lead and sparked the cultural/sexual revolution that continues to impact society today with their mantra of free love, no fault divorce, disconnecting sexual activity from procreation, which then led to abortion rights, same sex marriage and will eventually lead to eradicating the legal differences between male and female and all gender identity if culture continues in the present trajectory.

Until the church begins to make disciples with a biblical worldview in all of the major cultural mountains, the humanists will rule the philosophy of life, and culture will continue its downward spiral towards social chaos and political tyranny.

## *Political Theory*

Out of a philosophy of life comes a political theory that attempts to codify their beliefs into systems of government, law and policy. Cultural elites begin asking themselves the questions "How shall we now govern in light of our prevailing philosophy of life?"

## *Public Policy and Law*

Out of the prevailing political theory, cultural elites ask themselves the question, "In light of our political theory, what laws should we enact that are congruent with our political theory?"

For example, Socialists, Marxists and Communists in theory will attempt to enact policies that marginalize religion by keeping it out of the public square; they will defund family dynasties by the inheritance tax, and they will use tax monies to indoctrinate young children via public school education. This is also why those with a socialistic view believe that a large central government should leverage the most power over all of the other jurisdictions, (individual govt., family govt., business, and church) and that a large, central (federal) government is the answer for all social ills.

So, if believers once again become the cultural elites and have to enact laws and public policy they have to ask themselves the question, "by whose standard of ethics should we govern?"

Most evangelical Christians have no biblical template to answer this question beyond their goal of affecting change in the cultural mountains. But by what standard of ethics and law do we affect change in society? If we do not use the biblical model, we have no other choices except the teachings of the Greek/Roman philosophers, and the secular humanists which by default is the only positions for political theory and law believers have if they have not taken seriously the Mosaic law, (which I believe is the only standard of law and ethics Christians should use to disciple gatekeepers who will in turn disciple and build nations).

# CHAPTER SEVEN

# THE LAW OF GOD DEFINED

Many scholars believe that there are three major components of the Law of God: **Ceremonial Law, Moral Law, Civic Law.**

### Ceremonial Law

Ceremonial law is made up of the Levitical System of the priesthood. This involves making a covenant with God via circumcision; the five different types of animal sacrifices that caused God to cover personal and national sin; ceremonial laws involving clean and unclean animals, humans and things that the Jews were commanded to touch not, taste not; as well as keeping the Jubilee every fifty years and the three major feasts. All this has been done away with in Christ. This is why John the Baptist called Jesus the Lamb of God who takes away the sins of the world (John 1:29). This is also probably the main thing the New Testament writers were referring to when they were continually alluding to the fact that they were then living in the last days. They most likely meant The Last Days of the Levitical System and sacrificial structure. Otherwise, they would be false prophets because Jesus said this generation would not pass away until all these things He prophesied were fulfilled (Matthew 24:34). Within one generation of His crucifixion the Levitical systems, the temple as well as the genealogical records of the tribes were destroyed in A.D. 70 under the Roman invasion Jesus predicted in Luke 21:20. We need to understand the context of these and other passages such as Hebrews 10:25-28 and Acts 2:17 which most likely refer to the last days of the Jewish nation and Levitical system.

## *Moral Law*

The Moral law is made up of The Ten Commandments given to Moses at Mt. Sinai. These ten laws are trans-historical, trans-cultural, multi-generational and applicable to every culture and ethnic group throughout history because they are rooted in the original created order since they are a reflection of the nature and character of God. Some erroneous doctrines such as anti-nominalism, hyper-dispensational and hyper-grace teachings say these commandments are no longer necessary. However, every one of the Ten Commandments is repeated in the gospels and the epistles of the New Testament. Consequently, The Ten Commandments serve as the New-Testament standard for sanctification. The law cannot save us - it is only the standard of ethics the Holy Spirit uses to sanctify us (read Romans 8:3,4). The first four set the tone for the rest of the commandments and are given in the order of importance. These initial four show our obligation towards God and the last six commandments have to do with our obligation to our neighbor. This is a framework for discipling a nation; the context of Exodus 20 shows that these commandments are primarily a framework for national prosperity. Those in the body of

Christ without a biblical worldview miss this point and believe these Ten commands are merely a moral code for individual believers. This is what happens when a person doesn't start off with the cultural mandate found in Genesis 1:26-28 as their interpretive grid. Without the goal of bringing God's influence to the created order, a person is only left with an individual moral code. As regarding our nation, right now I believe we need to focus on the last six commandments having to do with our extracting public policy regulating how people are to live together, because our nation is too far gone to deal with the first four commandments. (That will be for the next two generations to deal with if indeed we begin to gain ground with the last six.) Consequently, each of the Ten Commandments are a category that is extrapolated in various ways and in various situations through the civic law. (Of course, if a national revival takes place and turns us back to putting God first , then it will be easier to deal with the last six commandments.)

## Civic Law

This is the 613 laws that take each of the ten categories and applies it in the context of the nation. We who disciple leaders that influence nations are called to extract principles by looking at these 613 laws and applying it to the sphere or domain those we train are assigned to serve. However, in regards to applying the Civic Law out of the Ten Commandments, we need to correctly divide the word of truth (2 Timothy 2:15). That is to say, we need to understand that some of the laws are not relevant because they only had to do with Israel. For example, the command to build a parapet on the roof of all houses

(Deut. 22:8) is no longer relevant but the principle of having safety measures so a person does not fall off the roof can still be applied today. Also the New Testament modified the penalties for breaking the law. There is no longer a death penalty mandated for sexual sins, blasphemy, idolatry, kidnapping, and rebellion. There is no clear consensus on whether the death penalty should be enforced at all. In most cases only Romans 13:1-7 seems to allude to God allowing civil government the right to use the sword as His minister but specific penalties are not discussed. Also, we have to remember that the same Roman government used the sword unlawfully to put Christians to death. Genesis 9:5-6 has been cited by some to declare the death penalty for murder since that law predated both testaments and was based in the created order relating to the fact that since humanity is made in the image of God, when someone sheds man's blood, from man shall his blood also be shed.

The reason why the death penalty is no longer mandated for adultery, homosexuality, and rebellion is because in the New Testament age we have the fullness of grace in Christ (John 1:17) and all people have a post-resurrection chance of being washed in the blood of Jesus, (something they did not have the opportunity to experience in the First Testament). Furthermore, in this testament we are not only forgiven, but we are born again in the Holy Spirit and transformed from within, which makes believers a new creation (2 Cor. 5:17) something believers could not experience before the resurrection of Christ. Also, the apostle Paul in Romans chapter one cited homosexuality, idolatry, covetousness, envy, greed, backbiting and disobedience to parents all in the same category; thus, if homosexuals should get the death penalty and be penalized, then all of us in the body of Christ are also in trouble because we are guilty of the other sins mentioned in the same context. Paul said at the end of Romans chapter one that those who practice such things are worthy of death, but he never calls for the death penalty. Also, the man caught in an adulterous relationship with his father's wife in 1 Corinthians 5 would be guilty of the death penalty mentioned in Leviticus chapter 18, but in 2 Corinthians, Paul the apostle pleads with the church to receive this man back into the fold and in neither letter does he call for the death penalty, just that he put out of the church. Furthermore, in 1 Corinthians chapter 6 Paul says that some of the members of the church were homosexual offenders before they were saved but now they were saved and washed in the blood. Nowhere does he call for the death penalty! (1 Cor 6:9-11) Finally, in John chapter 8, Jesus said of the women caught in adultery to go and sin no more - He never called for the death penalty even though He was without sin and could have cast the first stone at her! (John 8:1-8) Also in the same chapter, (8:17) He also says that He and His Father serve as two witnesses –which in context meant that they could have served as judicial witnesses to throw the first stone at the woman in the beginning of the same chapter (the same woman He commanded to "sin no more"- thus, knowing as a divine witness that she was in fact guilty of adultery). So, it is obvious to me that the New Testament modifies the penalties of the Law without compromising the moral ethics of the law; the church has a choice, either apply the principles of the civic law as extracted out of the Ten

Commandments or revert back to the civic law philosophies of the Greeks and Romans. The law of God or the law of men - that is the choice for discipling nations, and I, for one, choose the law of God!

# CHAPTER EIGHT

# APPLYING THE LAW OF GOD IN CULTURE

Although we can get ideas and extrapolate principles regarding the application of the moral law to culture from the 613 civic laws, it is important we also attempt to see how the Ten Commandments can affect present day public policy. Because the Ten Commandments are not the sole focus of this book, I will just use a few of the Ten Commandments to show that they are still relevant to public policy today.

For example, the first commandment, which has to do with having no other gods before the Lord, cannot be forced upon a pluralistic society in the same way it was during the days of Israel because in the New Covenant, we do not force conversions by the sword or by the law. The best that we can do is to favor the One True God in our laws and culture (in the same way the original twelve states in the USA did in their respective constitutions), but showing favor and forcing conversions are two different things. The fourth commandment regarding the keeping of the Sabbath can be applied by not allowing excess commercialism to take place on Sundays as well as having laws protecting workers from being fired for refusing to work on Sundays so they can attend church services. The sixth commandment forbidding murder can easily be applied to forbid abortion and federally defund Planned Parenthood. God hates the shedding of innocent blood (Proverbs 6:17) and pre-birth murder is condemned in scripture as much as post-birth murder (the civil law is specific in it's condemnation of causing a pre-birth death of an infant; read Exodus 21:22-24). Along with this command not to murder is the fact that a human being has been made in the image of God, which makes it a gross crime to kill such a living thing! (Because it is akin to killing the similitude of God Himself as Genesis 9:5,6 says.) Since all humans are image bearers of God, they are born with innate dignity, which gives us a view of the sanctity of human life. This view also makes a strong cause for human rights which can be used against human trafficking, racism and all forms of inequity. The sixth commandment forbidding adultery, like the other commands, is a category for all sexual sins according to Leviticus 18, which lumps adultery, homosexuality, bestiality, and incest together under the rubric of sexual sin. (Hence it is wrong when the church focuses on homosexuality more then heterosexual sin like adultery.) The eighth commandment forbidding theft can be applied to the central government extracting excess taxes from individuals, families and businesses. It also implies that God has granted humans the right to own private property because how can a person steal without the concept of an individual's right to ownership! This shoots a hole in the theory of the Christians who promote communism in the name of Christianity! The ninth commandment dealing with not bearing false witness can be applied to having a just and equitable judicial process as well as being against corrupting the law through bribes, witness tampering and by lying about others for the sake of selfish gain through lawsuits. Finally, the last commandment forbidding covetousness is an indictment against those who (out of envy) want to force egalitarianism upon our culture and impose equality through the forced redistribution of wealth. The bible teaches that justice is based on affording people an equal opportunity, not necessarily equal pay. Nations should have laws that promote a meritocracy (pay based on merit, skill and problem solving) not an entitlement mentality!

# CHAPTER NINE

# HOW JESUS SUMMARIZED THE LAW

When someone asked Jesus the Messiah what the greatest commandment was, He did not hesitate and said that there were two laws that summarized all the other laws. He said that the greatest commandment was to love the Lord our God with all our heart, mind and soul and strength; the second is like it, in that, you shall love your neighbor as yourself. On these two commandments the whole law hangs (Matthew 22:27-30). Thus, Jesus summarized the Ten Commandments and 613 civic laws in these two categories. The first four commandments prioritize our obligation to God and the last six prioritize our relationship with our neighbor. So, Jesus seemed to view both the Ten Commandments and the civic law in these two categories.

CHAPTER TEN

# HOW WE CAN IMITATE JESUS FOR SOCIETAL TRANSFORMATION

Truly, the bible tells us that we were chosen by God primarily to be conformed to the image of His Son Jesus (romans 8:29,30). That being said, our righteousness is in Jesus, who fulfilled the law through His perfect life (read Romans 10:4; Matthew 5:17; 2 Corinthians 5:21). Nobody can follow the law exactly, because through the law is the knowledge of sin (Romans 3:20). The only way a person can be saved is through faith in Jesus Christ, who fulfilled all the righteousness of the law for those who believe in Him (Romans 8:3-4). Hence, we are not only to understand His life in the context of his last few hours on the cross, but we need to understand that righteousness was fulfilled through the totality of His life. Consequently, we are to study and imitate His whole life, not just believe in Him for salvation. All the law and the prophets pointed to the life and ministry of the Lord Jesus Christ (Luke 24:44).

So, it is incumbent upon us to understand not only how He fulfilled the whole law but also how He alone is the consummation of the plan of God at the end of human history (Ephesians 1:9-11).

This is why Jesus described Himself in three ways: He said in John 14:6 I am: **The Way, The Truth, The Life.** If we are going to fulfill the commandment God gave to the first Adam to influence the created order (in Genesis 1:26-28), then we need to *imitate* the last Adam (1 Cor. 15:45).

Only transformed people can transform society! We cannot only imitate the ministry of Christ; we have to imitate the character of Christ. This is why, before Jesus commanded His people to function as the salt of the earth and the light of the world (Matthew 5:13-16), He gave them the ideals of how to live in what is known as the "Beatitudes". (Matthew 5:1-12). This shows us that God wants His people to go through a process that crushes our strong will so that we live like Christ out of our humility and brokenness. Truly, God surrounds power with problems and challenges so that, by the time we have the power and the position we don't really want it anymore! If you desire power, then you are probably not ready for it yet! We look at the product (salt and light) but God views the process of brokenness and humility as more important then the product because He desires more then anything else, that we act and live like the Lord Jesus. So, we need to study this section in Matthew 5:1-12 which I believe is part of a section containing the greatest summation of the character of Christ in the whole bible. Most of us (including me) would love to bypass Matthew 5:1-12 and jump right into Matthew 5:13-16 regarding our functioning as Salt and Light . However, before we are ready for influence, we need to go through the grid and process of the challenges in life (that breaks our pride) so we can eventually conform to the image and character of Christ.

## The Way of Jesus

The way of Jesus has to do with imitating the life and character of Jesus.

## The Beatitudes

2   *And he opened his mouth and taught them, saying:*

3   "Blessed are the poor in spirit, for theirs is the kingdom of heaven.

4   "Blessed are those who mourn, for they shall be comforted.

5   "Blessed are the meek, for they shall inherit the earth.

6   "Blessed are those who hunger and thirst for righteousness, for they shall be satisfied.

7   "Blessed are the merciful, for they shall receive mercy.

8   "Blessed are the pure in heart, for they shall see God.

9   "Blessed are the peacemakers, for they shall be called sons* of God.

10  "Blessed are those who are persecuted for righteousness' sake, for theirs is the kingdom of heaven.

11  "Blessed are you when others revile you and persecute you and utter all kinds of evil against *you falsely on my account. 12 Rejoice and be glad, for your reward is great in heaven, for so they persecuted the prophets who were before you. (Taken from the ESV bible)*

### Blessed are the Poor in Spirit

The poor in spirit are those who know within themselves that without Christ they are nothing, and that they are impoverished apart from the grace and love of God. They are poor, not because they are financially poor but because they continually realize they are spiritually poor. As a result, they are always craving a greater and deeper knowledge of God. Compared to Christ they know they have not arrived and will never have it all apart from Him. They will always be poor compared to the inexhaustible riches of Christ!

### Blessed are Those who Mourn

Those who mourn are those who can place themselves in the universe of another person so as to feel their pain, sorrow, and even to suffer with them and for them. It is not the same as feeling sorry for them or having sympathy; it is more like empathy. Before God uses a leader for His kingdom purposes, he wants to work empathy inside of them so they can express His heart and mind towards others, which only comes from understanding their pain. Mourning also has to do with being grieved over the sin of others. Instead of being a self-righteous judge, God is calling us to grieve, to intercede and to groan in the spirit for the sins of our nation and those around us. God cannot fully trust a leader who doesn't have His heart and mind towards others.

### Blessed are the Meek, for They Shall Inherit the Earth

The meek are those who have the kindness and gentleness of Christ at work inside of them. (Psalm 18:35). They are not the loud and boisterous leaders who point to themselves and brag about their achievements. It is the person who humbly serves in the background that God lifts up to inherit the land. This is a very important passage because often times the 'activists' in the body of Christ put down the 'pietists' who embrace humility (and the deeper life) because they say they are not practical and are too mystical; the 'pietists' often put down the 'activists' (both do not understand each other in most cases!) because they say they are full of wrong motives and fleshly ambition but this passage connects both camps. Truly, according to Jesus, we cannot have influence and be salt and light unless we are meek. We, in the camp that espouse the message of the Kingdom and cultural transformation, need to learn to embrace the deeper contemplative life of the mystics and those who are self aware -as well as the teachings related to the seven mountain mandate. If not, then the very thing we strive for (to inherit the land) will elude us because we have not allowed the character of Christ to be formed on the inside of us.

## Blessed are Those who Hunger and Thirst for Righteousness

The greatness of God is so great that we can never have enough of Him! Jesus taught us in this passage that only those that are continually hungry will be filled. It is paradoxical because you have to be hungry to be filled and if you are filled, then you will go away empty (Luke 6:25). God wants to have leaders raised up that crave for His righteousness to be expressed on the earth (through His laws and His ways, influencing the systems of nations) as well as hungering to know Him personally (Jeremiah 9:23,24).

## *Blessed are the Merciful, for They will Receive Mercy*

Mercy has to do with treating a person better then they deserve. Jesus's death demonstrated God's mercy toward us, in that He saved us from our sins even though we did not deserve it (Luke 1:50). Since God treats His children with mercy, He expects us to do the same with those who don't deserve it or who mistreat us (Luke 6:35,36).

This is in contrast to many of the Christian leaders who constantly sound judgmental in their denunciations against sin and who misrepresent the love of God to this fallen world. To be clear, God's mercy is demonstrated even in the common grace He displays to His creatures when He sends the sun and the rain on both the just and the unjust (Matthew 5:45). When in doubt (whether to show a person mercy or judgment), show mercy, since mercy triumphs over judgment! (Read James 2:13)

## *Blessed are the Pure in Heart, for They Shall See God*

The pure in heart are not those that are sinless, but those who are sincere and have the right motive before God. Too many leaders have a hidden agenda and want to do great things to pad their pockets or to receive glory from men. The Lord is raising up leaders whose only motive is the glory of God and the advance of His Kingdom!

Those who have the right motives and who have a heart after God will have the clearest picture of the character and nature of God. Only those who truly know

God will be able to make Him known. I have seen it over and over again the past thirty years, that those leaders who have the wrong motives in regards to ministry will eventually be found out by others and they will greatly limit their leadership capacity.

## Blessed are the Peacemakers because They will be Called the Children of God

The peacemakers are those with the unique ability to understand opposing views as well as the proponents of said opposing idea- even if they, themselves don't agree with their viewpoint. Peacemakers are able to get into the universe of other people (for a fusion of horizons), see the common goals of opposing parties, and have the godly wisdom to bring reconciliation and in some cases even synthetization! Leaders with this particular calling are gifted statesmen and ambassadors, and are very effective in ecumenical endeavors and even inter-faith initiatives.

People will call these people the 'children of God' because of the great intuition and insight they have to bring enemies together and even to get them to love one another and work together. We need more statesmen and ambassadors in the body of Christ so we can reveal the love and power of God to those of different religions and ideologies and become the top gatekeepers in a pluralis-tic society. Truly, I believe this gift is primarily used for the civil arena in contemporary times, although it can be used even in a family or church squabble. This is per-haps the most misunderstood and unappreciated calling in the body of Christ but perhaps the most appreciated in the geo-political world (Nelson Mandella, Ghandi,

Martin Luther King are examples of those who have been used as peacemakers in their respective nations).

Those who are in the body of Christ and are called to serve as peacekeepers also need to understand the doctrine of Common Grace, in which God blesses the world of both the saved and the unsaved with His bounty. God even calls unsaved civil magistrates His 'deacons' in Romans 13:4, as well as calling an unbelieving King named Cyrus His chosen, anointed servant who will fulfill all of His purposes (read Isaiah 45,46). This doctrine is important because it will give the peacekeeper theological insight and permission to work for the common good of secular cities (read Jeremiah 29:1-13) as well as working closely with civic leaders who may not know the Lord personally for salvation, yet are His servants who do His will in nations and cities.

## Blessed are Those Who are Persecuted for Righteousness Sake

Any person who is going to be a leader has to have thick-skin and be willing to be spoken against and be misrepresented. God allows this to happen with His choice servants because He is testing them at times to show them whether they are in ministry for the praise of men or for the praise of God. If a leader is doing it for the praise of men, then they will want to resign and find another assignment once things heat up and get ugly.

In order to be the leader God has called us to be, we need to die to self, take up our cross and be willing to suffer with and for Christ even as He suffered for us.

God wants to raise up leaders who love His righteousness more then their own life, liberty and freedom.

Perhaps those with the greatest rewards in the Kingdom of Heaven are those who make the ultimate sacrifice and lose their physical life for the sake of the gospel! The world will be changed, not by men who are willing to live, but by those who are willing to die for His purposes.

## The Truth

The truth of Jesus is simply summed up in Ephesians 1:9-11 which in essence, is the Lordship of Christ over all of creation.

This one sentence in Ephesians sums up the purpose of the kingdom of God and the meta-narrative of scripture "That all things, both in heaven and earth will be united together in Christ. Jesus cries out and claims every square inch of the world and says "mine" (so said Abraham Kuyper). If Jesus is not Lord over every thing, He is not Lord at all. For example, if someone can prove that mathematics is outside the scope of the Lordship of Christ then they have, in essence, proven that Jesus is not the true Messiah.

So, the truth of Jesus is the fact that He came to the earth to be the King of kings and Lord of lords (Rev. 19:16, John 18:37). He did not merely come to be a savior but He came to prepare the world to receive Him back as the only true potentate and ruler of the universe. This is why Christian leaders who desire to reach all of the mountains of culture need to acquire a biblical worldview so that we will understand how to align every domain in this world under the Lordship of Christ. If we do not have a biblical worldview in disciplines like History, Science, Math, Politics, Law, Family, Philosophy,

Economics, Media, Arts, Entertainment, etc., then how do we expect to disciple nations?!

The major theme of both the first and second testament is the Kingdom of God, which means the 'King's domain'. Thus, the Kingdom can only be applied to the earth through understanding and preaching the truth, which is personified in Jesus who is Lord of all creation.

### The Life

The life of Jesus shows that apart from Him we can do nothing. We are not going to reach this world through mere strategies, and church growth initiatives. Zechariah 4:7 says, "Not by power or by might but by my spirit says the Lord".

Jesus said in John 15 that if we do not abide in Him we would be like a branch that no longer abides in the vine and who eventually dies and is burned in the fire.

Those of us who preach the kingdom cannot forsake our biblical roots of fasting, prayer, and moving in the gifts of the Holy Spirit and the power of God to demonstrate the resurrection to the world. Those who preach the kingdom actually need to fast and pray even more then those who merely preach the individual gospel of salvation because we are now dealing with archetypes and principalities over nations. These high level demonic hosts hide behind political, economic and ideological systems (2 Corinthians 10:3-5) whose only threat is the truth of Jesus who claims every major social system in the world as His. Those who preach only on salvation and individual redemption will only face individual demons who come into people, but those who demonstrate and apply the principles of the Kingdom in cities will deal with Satanic hierarchies ruling empires (read Daniel chapter 10 and Ephesians 6:10-13).

As a result, I usually have almost fifty personal mature intercessors praying for me every time I take a major ministry trip that involves training leaders in the church and the marketplace concerning the things of the Kingdom. This is also why I usually spend far more time seeking God and travailing in prayer then I do studying books because, unless my spiritual level of power is strong, I will not be able to stand against all of the pressures and tests that come my way because of my assignment. So in closing, we need to know the truth of Jesus but also the life and power of Jesus if we are gong to succeed in bringing His Kingdom on the earth as it is in heaven.

## *To summarize my findings:*

- We have One Kingdom Mountain that houses the church (Isaiah 2:2-4, Colossians 1:13);
- Out of which the church sends and equips leaders (Ephesians 4:11,12);
- To go into the seven major mountains of culture (Isaiah 2:2-4);
- Which are governed by the five jurisdictions (Personal, Family, Business, Civic, Church);
- Which eventuate into the four steps needed to form public policy and law (Theology leads to a philosophy of life which leads to political theory which leads ultimately to policy and law);
- Policy and law has to refer back to the Moral Law of God codified in 10 Commandments if we are going to be biblical (Exodus 20);

- The 10 commandments are extrapolated and applied in civic society by 613 laws (as found in Exodus, Leviticus, Numbers and Deuteronomy);
- These 10 laws are summarized by two laws (Matthew 22:37-40) which are totally fulfilled by one man (Jesus);
- Who alone is the way, the truth, and the life (John 14:6).

In closing, my hope is, that through this book, I was able to weave together both testaments, including the Mosaic Law and the 'Beatitudes', both piety and policy, and show that being empowered by the person and power of Christ is the only way we will experience true transformation, both, individually and in the nations.

Additional teachings and resources by
Dr. Joseph Mattera, can be found
at www.josephmattera.org


740 40TH STREET
BROOKLYN NY 11232, USA
718.436.0242 EXT. 13
INFO@JOSEPHMATTERA.ORG


**Facebook:** /josephmattera
**Twitter:** /josephmattera
**YouTube:** /josephmattera
**Instagram:** /joseph_mattera

## μ65

Powered by eGenCo

Generation Culture Transformation
Specializing in publishing for generation culture change

Visit us Online at:
www.micro65.com

Write to: eGenCo
824 Tallow Hill Road
Chambersburg, PA 17202, USA
Phone: 717-461-3436
Email: info@micro65.com

facebook.com/egenbooks
youtube.com/egenpub
egen.co/blog
pinterest.com/eGenDMP
twitter.com/eGenDMP
instagram.com/egenco_dmp

56451268R00042